D1240629

DEDICATION

This book is dedicated to all who have failed and made a decision that your current state was NOT your final state. This is for all the students who have been deemed hopeless and set out to make those statements a fallacy. I was once counted out and found a way to place the bet on myself and win big-time… You can do the same and more. Despite what other people say to you in your life, you are only as great as YOU think you are.

"You have to paint the picture for the people. Don't give inartistic people the brush and easel to determine your masterpiece."

- Alfred Blake

THIS IS AN I AM MULTI LLC BOOK

PUBLISHED BY ALFRED E. BLAKE

The Students Handbook To Breaking All The Rules can be purchased wholesale for educational, business, or sales promotional use. For information please email Iammultipr@gmail.com

Published in Roselle, NJ 07203 by Alfred E. Blake,

Library of Congress Cataloging-In-Publication Data available on request

The Students Handbook To Breaking All The Rules

ISBN: 978-0-578-08598-2

Printed in the United States September 2011

Available for speaking engagements, seminars and workshops. View book details at www.webreakrules.com

READ THIS BOOK, and you'll be RICH!!!

Okay, I'll be Rich too. Live and learn that this is the way the world works. You help me and I'll help you (Winks).

ON a serious note:

Breaking All The Rules... is a practical application of 52 rules that need to be broken if you plan on succeeding in life. This 52-week journey embodies the essence of developing an attitude built for the obstacles that EVERY successful person has endured and overcome. If you read AND apply the rule-breakers weekly and record your practical application in your life, you will improve and be armed with the tools that are necessary for success through cultivation of the mind.

There are a minimum of two rules to be broken with EVERY decision that you will make. Ultimately the difference between the successful person and unsuccessful person lies in the rules they decided to break. Breaking All The Rules is a yearlong journey with Original axioms and philosophies to propel you to a higher knowledge of Breaking All The Rules and excelling by making proper decisions and adopting a positive attitude. For years we have been told that we are to follow all the rules. This is false. Attention and acclaim have ALWAYS been given to Rule Breakers and defiers of social norms. You have to decide whose rules are most advantageous to break. This book will teach you how to do that.

Everyone who reads this book will learn the power of being unique, how to believe in the talents that they possess, and overall it will further develop the character of the reader. This book will teach you to recognize, develop, and believe that you can and WILL win in life. Overall you will become an alumnus of Breaking All The Rules, and be many steps closer to attaining success.

Instructions on how to navigate book:

VERY IMPORTANT!

POST rule-breaking quotes on Twitter, Facebook, Tumblr, bus stops, bathroom stalls in every public bathroom that you visit and EVERYWHERE ELSE... WEEKLY (I am not in any way promoting vandalism but rather empowerment sharing)! Share the wealth of knowledge with friends and family!

How to navigate book: Each week there is a concept that will be grasped. Each chapter includes a rule that is detrimental to your livelihood and a Rule Breaker (original quote/philosophy) to reverse the effects of that rule. After those items are read, the breakdown will explain the key concept. Upon reading, make sure to apply the rule breaker to your life, and record in the notes section how you have applied the rule to your life.

Link To Life Exercises: are included in each chapter. These exercises are used to give you direct application of lessons in your life. In order to receive the full benefit of each chapter it is mandatory that you complete each Link To Life (L2L) exercise and answer questions honestly. Each L2L exercise has a new word and questions that are to be answered at the end of each chapter. Each Link to life exercise will embed the knowledge in your brain and more importantly help you to positively change your daily habits. It will also make you more astute!

Notes: The notes section in each chapter is for you to note how you have applied the rule breaker in your life and the way you were affected by application. The more detailed you are, the more you will reap from each rule-breaker. No matter how inspired and enthused you become, the Rule Breaker is USELESS without APPLICATION!!!

YOU HAVE EVERYTHING YOU NEED TO WIN!

Have you ever seen or encountered a person who felt they weren't good enough to accomplish a task or overcome an obstacle? Your answer is undoubtedly yes! However, you will not be put in the same category! Before you embark on this journey to a fuller, happier, more productive you, first you must realize that you have everything you need to win. The first step in your journey to doing so is realizing that you were born uniquely perfect. Look at yourself in the mirror... Do you see anyone who looks, talks, behaves and thinks exactly like you? Exactly... I didn't think so. In order to achieve the win, you must truly believe that your unique qualities are your strengths.

I did not always have the knowledge of having everything I needed to win. It was the 2003 season of the illustrious Pine Forge basketball team. This was the most important game that we'd ever played in our lives. We were up against a giant stacked team. 75 percent of the team was recruited from around the country and the other 25 percent from outside of the country. We weren't involved in a challenge; we had a battle on our hands! Since we knew what was at stake, we had two choices: to take up the challenge, or hide under a rock.

Can you guess what we did? We decided that we were going to play our hearts out. It was twenty-nine seconds left! Fans were cheering excitedly, girls screamed their favorite player's names and chaperones transformed from teachers to unruly spectators! Through all the madness, the Game clock hovered over us like a warden in a maximum-security prison. We wanted not only to win, but also leave with a legacy for defeating one of the most dominant feeder schools for NCAA teams that you watch during March Madness! Breathing was frantic...It felt impossible for our hearts to be held hostage by skin and ribs alone. This was the most important game of our lives.... Losing was not an option. As we glanced at the scoreboard, it read Pine Forge Academy 89, American International H.S. 92.

As I glared over at the opposing sideline, my eyes saw the 6'8 and 6'6 towers… Waiting to get back in the game! I said to myself…. "I will not lose, I will jump out of the gym to get these rebounds, and The Bigger they are the harder they fall. So naturally, I was aiming for their knees!"

Coach screamed time-out! During the time-out, we looked to our coach for instructions. He said: This is our game! All we need to do is make this stop and score! He instructed us to play a man-to-man defense and focus on boxing out the two towers under the hoop!

Before my team headed back out, coach had us huddle up. He gave us three chants that unknowingly would change my life and yours forever. The first chant was (who is Going to Win?) We responded…. We are!" He then chanted, (how bad do you want it!) We responded, real bad! The Third chant was, (what are you going to do to get that win!) We said… execute!

Before I tell you the outcome of the game, I will share with you the lesson that will change your life. The Three chants that we rehearsed in the huddle have great value. The first chant highlights Realization. Your brain reacts to your thoughts. Realization is the first step to any accomplishment. I can never sell you a single thing, unless I realize its worth. As people, we do most things backwards…we eat a salad as an appetizer rather that after our meal to help with digestion, we talk before we think, and we divorce before we die! Realization of your greatness is the first step in being successful in anything. Later in life I realized that coach was giving us more than advice to win a game, but also the advice needed to win in the game of life. The three things that you need to win lie within yourself. The three necessities are realization, desire and being able to execute a plan to win.

The life-changing rule breakers in this book will help you to realize your potential, Stimulate your desire to win and help your plans become reality through execution! *Read, and share with a friend!*

GREATNESS COMES AFTER FAME AND BEING
RECOGNIZED FOR MY WORK.

"Greatness is not acquired,
it is realized."
- Kasan Lane

Say this affirmation as loud as you possibly can: I AM GREAT YOU'RE JUST LATE! Most have been trained to conceal their greatness as a way of being humble or modest. While I do not suggest running around town wildly brandishing a sign that says, "I am the greatest of all time." I do suggest telling yourself that you are truly great. There is a misconception that greatness comes after accolades and accomplishments. Most of those accolades never appear because most do not accept their genius first! Summertime as a child before summer jobs and car insurance, you are able to enjoy nature and the beauty that it effortlessly provides. Rewind the hands of time and think of a time when you were challenged to find a four-leaf clover. While I remember searching many times, I NEVER remember finding any. Four leaf clovers are said to be lucky and extremely rare. When you search throughout the meadow, upon finding a four-leaf clover you feel as though you will be able to conquer the world due to your acquisition and the rare nature of four-leaf clovers. In life, you are that four-leaf clover. No matter how hard I search, I will never find another you. While there is no greatness in a four-leaf clover, there is something special in you. Every human being is a four-leaf clover, most just cut off the fourth leaf. Don't wait for someone else to proclaim you great. Remember you must say daily: "I'm Great, you're just late" and you will see the world move to your rhythm.

"You are not to act like an artist, not to walk like an artist, or even dress like an artist, you must think like one. Everything starts with a thought. All great things among mankind were conceived in the confines of the mind as a mere idea. Your thoughts become your words, your words become your actions, and your actions become your life. More important than the lifestyle is the mentality. Greatness is a mentality that if adopted will propel you in life to places unimaginable."

- Kasan Lane

Define Unrivalled.

What is great about you? Note to self: If you don't know how will anybody else know?

Now that you know what makes you great, what will you choose to do with your time on earth change the lives of others?

What changes have you made this year and what others will you make? As a result, how will you change for the better? What are your first steps?

I CAN REACH MY DESIRED DESTINATION
WHILE KEEPING THE SAME PEOPLE AROUND
ME. EVERYONE IN MY CIRCLE IS MEANT TO
TRAVEL WITH ME THROUGHOUT MY LIFE-LONG
JOURNEY.

RULE BREAKER

"When you change your destination, your environment has to change as well."

This quote comes from the person that your parents always instructed you to stay away from! I was part of the crowd that was always in the principal's office, always in fights and always attracting negative attention. While I thought I was doing the "cool" thing to lead me to popularity, it was actually leading me down the road to FAILURE! Once my destination changed to success, so did the activities I was involved with and bad influences in my life! As you progress in your journey called life, you must always evaluate the individuals whom you allow into your circle. While they may have longevity, they may lack value. When you analyze your friends, you should see a direct correlation to your desired destination in life. Do not be misconstrued; I am not saying that all your friends should have the same goals, but rather similar attitudes towards life. If you look at your circle and they are not focused, you owe it to yourself to update your roster of friends.

"Leaving unmotivated friends is never a betrayal of the friend, but rather staying is a betrayal of yourself"
- Alfred Blake

Define assimilation.

_____

_____

_____

_____

_____

What is your destination? How must you change your environment to make your destination reachable?

_____

_____

_____

_____

_____

Why is sacrifice so important in your development as a member of society?

_____

_____

_____

_____

_____

What habits need to change in order for your environment to change?

_____

_____

_____

_____

RULE BREAKER

"Conquering the fear of being alone is the beginning of conquering the world."

Many people are under the false assumption that it is more beneficial to follow the trends rather than basking in your own aroma. The common misconception is that people who are extremely individualistic (on their own) get ostracized. A common axiom used is "One is the loneliest number." While one may be a lonely number, it is also a number of power, affluence and influence. There is one king, president and ONLY one you. Take pride in your idiosyncrasies! When you are able to accept yourself, your core values and your uniqueness, you are able to conquer the world. Look at Kanye West, Pink, Pharrell Williams, Madonna and Outkast. All of these artists have conquered so much ground due to their individuality! What will you do and how will you stand out?

Define idiosyncrasy.

What is unique about you?

How can your individuality allow you to stand out and capitalize on the world?

Why is being unique powerful?

Highlight some of the ways that the aforementioned artists dared to be themselves.

THE BIGGER MY EGO, THE MORE ACCEPTED I
WILL BE. PEOPLE MUST KNOW THAT I KNOW I
AM THE BEST.

RULE BREAKER

*"Your ego is like blowing bubble gum!
Once it gets too big, it will explode
right in your face! Stay humble and
win the hearts of millions."*

When I was a youth, I did nothing but toot a horn that wasn't working! I bragged until my lungs were blue! In actuality, my ego was bigger than my talent. Bragging did nothing but annoyed friends and family, and made others detest me. Through losing relationships and suffering greatly, I realized the power of humility. If you are extremely good, others will let you know. I learned that lesson from losing opportunities and having doors closed in my face. You don't have to suffer the same fate. Today you must make the pledge to allow your actions to replace your words. Some examples of allowing actions to speak for themselves are Michael Jordan, Magic Johnson and Lebron James. These players never have to say a word about their athletic abilities. Lebron's actions and records speak for him. How will you allow your actions to speak for you?

Define hubris.

_____
_____
_____
_____
_____

Think of people in your class, and yourself! How does it make you feel when people's egos are bigger than their talent?

_____
_____
_____
_____
_____

Would you prefer to surround yourself with boastful or humble people? Why?

_____
_____
_____
_____
_____

Why will being humble help you to succeed throughout life?

_____
_____
_____
_____
_____

RULE #5

MY PARENTS DIDN'T FINISH COLLEGE, SO I
CANT DO WHAT THEY DIDN'T DO.

RULE BREAKER

"Brief doubt is a sign of sanity, but long term doubt is a sign of insanity, and lack of action!"

While your parents often serve as an example, they are not always "THE EXAMPLE" to follow. Education is golden. Education is one of the few things that you can acquire, and have it accrue interest over time. Think of attaining education like the ability to be able to get into certain clubs. Travel forward/backwards in time to the first time you were turned down at a club for entry. This is the same way you will feel if you have the ability to achieve great heights, but are turned down due to your lack of education! While you may feel intimidated, and have brief doubt about graduation, just realize that the only thing you have to do differently is ACT ON YOUR DREAMS! Go forward and attend school, and watch your degree work for you! This is a mandate of success!

Define mandate.

_____

_____

_____

_____

Ask your parent/guardian what they believe they could have accomplished if they'd acquired a higher level of education.

_____

_____

_____

_____

Which is more important intention or action? Why?

_____

_____

_____

_____

How will your circumstances change once you take more action in your life rather than focusing on doubt?

_____

_____

_____

_____

Why is brief doubt a sign of sanity?

_____

_____

_____

_____

RULE BREAKER

"Treat your mind like a vacuum. Absorb non-threatening debris, and filter out the components that are harmful to your core."

EVERY thought that enters your mind will have a huge adverse or positive effect on your life. Most people are under the impression that what enters their minds can be discarded easily. That is false information. Most people will say, "I have a firm grasp on ideas and I know reality from fiction." If there is no monitoring system you will be held back in life.

I absorbed all the wrong debris as a youth. I followed the steps of criminals, class clowns and people headed down the road to failure. The debris that I absorbed was ignorance. I consumed this harmful substance, because I was unaware of the effects it had on my core. In this scenario, your mind is your core. Be sure to constantly look for ways to improve yourself, strengthen your core and guard it closely. This is done through allowing the right ideas and philosophies to be adopted in your life. Those philosophies can be found in positive leaders through their actions and lifestyle.

Define filtration.

_____

_____

_____

_____

_____

What types of stimuli are harmful to your mind?

_____

_____

_____

_____

_____

What damage can you bring to your core with a group of negative friends?
What benefit can be reaped from positive friends?

_____

_____

_____

_____

_____

What can we put in our minds to promote positivity, knowledge, and ultimately growth?

_____

_____

_____

_____

NOTES

RULE #7

I CAN CHANGE SOMEONE EVEN IF THEY DON'T
WANT OR THINK THAT THEY NEED HELP.

RULE BREAKER

*"No matter how hard the doctor
tries, the CPR procedure is only
effective if the patient allows their
mouth to be opened."*

Have you ever heard the statement "you can lead a horse to water but cant make him drink"? If not, the statement means that you can lead and hint at what people should do in their lives, but they are going to do what they want regardless! You can give a person advice and the directions to the fountain of youth, but unless they accept them those directions are worthless to them! They say horses are stubborn and guess what...as human beings we are innately stubborn too! You, as a knowledgeable human being must realize that we all need help to survive! Allow others to help you! There are millions of resources at your grasp. Those resources are in your classrooms, neighborhoods and on the Internet. While there are millions of resources at your disposal, you must realize that the first step in achieving greatness is to accept and actively pursue help! As you are helped, never forget that it is your responsibility to help others as well. We cannot make it alone!

Define innate.

_____

_____

_____

_____

_____

Why must we allow others to help us in life?

_____

_____

_____

_____

When are we accepting too much help? How do you know?

_____

_____

_____

_____

Why is it important for you to not only accept help, but also help yourself?

_____

_____

_____

_____

NOTES

RULE #8

LIVING IN THE FAST LANE IS THE MOST PRODUCTIVE
LIFE! THE MONEY, CARS AND FAST LIFESTYLE IS THE
WAY TO LIVE.

RULE BREAKER

*"Water is at its clearest when it is
still. Mimic the water and clear
your mind through solitude. Then
record your thoughts."*

Life moves at the speed of light for most of us. Can you tell me how fast that is? I doubt you can! I just want you to know that it is too fast for you to enjoy the full potential of your days! Take time to invest in yourself and reflect!!! With the Internet, fast food restaurants and downloadable movies it is easy to go faster than you are meant to go. We often go so fast that we fail to recognize S.T.O.P. (Something That Orders Precaution). These signs are present in our relationships, health habits and adopted mind-set. If not careful, and you choose to blatantly disregard S.T.O.P. signs, they will slow you down, and adversely affect your well-being. Take the time to accept and correct S.T.O.P. signs in your life. My uncle works at the DMV. One day I asked him why most people fail their driving test, he replied, "They don't pay attention to S.T.O.P. signs". Once you fail to adhere to them, you are not only putting the lives of others at risk, but also the driver of the car (You) is put in unnecessary peril. Open your eyes and adhere to S.T.O.P signs or suffer greatly.

Define cognizant.

_____

_____

_____

_____

_____

What is the purpose of a S.T.O.P sign in life?

_____

_____

_____

_____

_____

Why is it important to stop and reflect on your life? What can you gain from taking the time to stop and evaluate? Give an example.

_____

_____

_____

_____

_____

Give examples of stop signs in life and daily relationships.

_____

_____

_____

_____

_____

RULE #9

I CAN HAVE FRIENDS THAT ARE ANGRY. THEY
WONT HAVE AN EFFECT ON MY BEHAVIOR
AND MY SPIRIT.

RULE BREAKER

"Stay away from angry people, for their wrath is as uncontrollable as a greased bowling ball tossed at you."

When is the last time you met an angry person that has control over their temper? The whole point of being labeled as angry is because that person has a LACK OF CONTROL over emotions! Think like this, Lack of control with a car creates accidents. While a human is not a car, they have access to cars and many more dangerous vehicles and objects that create massive damage! Why would you want to be around a person that is so uncontrollable and dangerous? I hope that gives you enough incentive to stay away from angry people who can operate vehicles that can cause mass damage (Random Rant/Run-on sentence). I know, I know, your thinking "Al how can I avoid them, angry psychotic people are like roaches in Alabama… They're EVERYWHERE". Guess what, you are right! Angry people surround you daily! However, you must promise not to allow their wrath to adversely affect you. Their anger is often times uncontrollable and will damper your spirit and harm you if you are in close proximity.

Dispel angry people from your circle…NOW! Anyone whom you allow to occupy your time should be one who adds value to you, and viceversa. Angry people are constantly a damper on your spirit and often times hard to control in their times of tantrum. If you have a tree surrounded by flames, it will surely burn and be destroyed. Do you want to be that tree? If your answer is yes, stay around those flames and be torched! If not, make a way to escape from the heat.

Define proximity.

_____
_____
_____
_____

Name a time in which anger has solved your problems? Share how choosing not to be angry has solved your problems.

_____
_____
_____
_____

Tell how your anger has adversely affected your life, or someone you know. Share how choosing not to be angry has solved your problems.

_____
_____
_____
_____

What could have been done differently in the previous situation?

_____
_____
_____
_____

RULE #10

I AM MOST PRODUCTIVE BY MYSELF. I DON'T NEED THE NEXT PERSON FOR SUCCEEDING. I AM GOOD ALL BY MYSELF.

RULE BREAKER

"Ants are so small, but build colossal colonies with respect to their size! Why? Because they work together! Have an ant's mindset and turn your "neighborhood" into your "Kingdom.""

You know the saying, "you came into the world alone and you'll leave alone"? That is an overused statement said by people who haven't learned how to mesh with others and work as a team. While that statement is partially true there's a piece of the pie missing! Those people conveniently delete the HUUUUUGE gap in between life and death (Depending on how well you were taught to look both ways when crossing the street). You need people and people need you! You are NOT alone!!!

Often times we blindly take the position of being alone in the world. You must open your eyes and dispel this misconception. In order to achieve maximal results, you must mimic the practices of ants! The secret to an ant colony and their success is their ability to delegate roles and perform with the utmost dignity and pride. Ants are able to work as a team and to share responsibilities. Look around you. There are people who possess skill sets that you do not. The key to any teams success is the ability to recognize roles and to execute. Whether you are the leader of the team or a role player, you will have to commit to a specific role. What role will you accept to uplift and turn your environment into a kingdom?

Define symbiotic.

_____

_____

_____

_____

Observe a sports team. How do the roles of each player differ and affect the outcome of the game?

_____

_____

_____

_____

Why is there strength in numbers? What is the difference in the effectiveness of a well-organized team, and an unorganized team? Explain.

_____

_____

_____

_____

How can you be of assistance to the people who are in your circle of friends in accomplishing their desired tasks?

_____

_____

_____

_____

NOTES

RULE #11

LIFE JUST HAPPENS, I USUALLY DON'T HAVE
CONTROL OVER WHAT HAPPENS.

RULE BREAKER

*"Treat life like an elevator, remember
that your choices are in front of you!
Know your destination and be ready
when you arrive!"*

When you go to a luxury apartment building there are typically a lot of floors and two levels that stand out. The first is the basement. When you think of the basement, what do you think of? The basement is typically a place where it is colder than most places in the building because of the lack of sunlight and proximity to the ground. There is no view and view is important because it opens your eyes to possibility. In the basement, you live with all the rodents and critters known as the "Undesirables". The basement is not where you want to be! Then there is the opposite of locations called the penthouse! The penthouse is a place with a lot of open space and possibility. Imagine a piano in the middle of the room, huge windows to view the city, an impeccable view to dance with the stars at night and rise with the sun. These are some of the options that are made available according to the choices you make on the elevator ride. Realize that EVERY decision is bringing you CLOSER or FURTHER from penthouse living.

Throughout my elevator ride called life, I have made many bad choices in my destination selection. Decisions such as choosing friends, whether or not to apply yourself in school and even how you monitor your food intake and health are all ways in which you determine the floor you will reach in life's elevator ride. The real question is: Do you want to live in the basement or do you wish to experience penthouse living?

Define echelon.

_____
_____
_____
_____
_____

An elevator will get you to any floor in the building! What can you do to ensure that you get to your correct destination?

_____
_____
_____
_____
_____

How do goals directly affect the choices you make in your elevator ride to success?

_____
_____
_____
_____
_____

What decisions do you regret making? What are the steps that you will take to correct them?

_____
_____
_____
_____
_____

NOTES

RULE #12

I HAVE DIFFERENT STANDARDS FROM MY FRIENDS, BUT
I'M NOT GOING TO BRING IT TO THEIR ATTENTION. I'LL
KEEP IT TO MYSELF.

RULE BREAKER

*"A man will never climb
Mount Everest with grease
soiled boots. Take a stand or fall
where you stand."*

You are taking steps to climbing a mountain of your own daily! Every hiker knows the importance of a sturdy climbing shoe! This is the difference between plummeting to your death, or rising to the occasion and overcoming the great feat of conquering a 19,341 foot high mountain (Kilimanjaro)! That mountain may be school, athletics, or even spiritual, but you cannot begin to progress until you take a stand for your beliefs and begin your voyage uphill! All great figures in history had to take a firm stance before they could ascend to the top of their respective fields. In closing, what will you stand for? The ability to take a stand signifies the ability to lead. The ability to lead means the gift of causing change in your life and the lives of others. Remember, to climb the heights your grip must be tight. "Take a stand or fall where you stand".

Define foundation.

_____

_____

_____

_____

Why is a foundation the most important part of any project?

_____

_____

_____

_____

What effect will a poor foundation have in comparison to a sturdy foundation?

_____

_____

_____

_____

What are three beliefs that you stand for and how will they help you to excel and benefit your community?

_____

_____

_____

_____

RULE #13

MY LIFE IS DISTRAUGHT BECAUSE OF
MY MOTHER/FATHER/HORRIBLE
BOYFRIEND/GIRLFRIEND.

RULE BREAKER

*"Prisoners are behind bars for a
reason. What is your reason for being
locked up in your self-made reality?"*

Rob someone, get sentenced for eight years. Possession of a gun four to six years minimum. Vehicular homicide 10-20 years behind bars. However, a mind with finite mentality is a lifetime sentence to mediocrity. For this one time, I am behooving you to think like a fugitive.

A fugitive is a prisoner who has escaped confinement. The sole goal of the individual is to do everything possible to evade the authorities. One action that all fugitives adopt is to run! When you are attempting to move past your current circumstances, you must choose to run towards your destiny. Continue to run until you have reached your final destination of success. If you stop, you surrender to mediocrity. If you surrender to mediocrity, you will be imprisoned to unhappiness and the prison guard will be the thought of "What if I would have".

Define mediocrity.

_____
_____
_____
_____
_____

List ways in which people can imprison themselves without committing a crime.

_____
_____
_____
_____
_____

Now think of ways to reverse the effects of self-imprisonment. What can you do to change your circumstance? Hints: (faith, habits, practice, changing mindset)

_____
_____
_____
_____

How do you prevent yourself from being imprisoned to mediocrity?

_____
_____
_____
_____

I CAN DRESS MYSELF UP TO MASK THE PAIN
I AM FEELING. I CAN IGNORE MY PROBLEMS AND FAKE
THE FUNK.

RULE BREAKER

"Masking your weaknesses is like licking your ashy lips in the winter! No matter how much you lick them, unless you treat the problem from the root, the condition will be worsened."

How many times have you been "Ashefied" in the winter with those dry, crusty smackers? When you have dry, ashy lips, it is an indicator of poor hydration. No matter how much outer moisture you apply, the lips will remain dry until you treat the core problem, and not just the surface. Every emotional issue that you undergo is based on an internal issue. While you may not be able to diagnose yourself, you should seek help from people such as guidance counselors and social workers. These people have your best interest in mind, and are necessary for you to recover from your issues. Do not be afraid of help. If a weakness is left untreated, you will never be able to see the strength that you possess beneath the surface. You must "Address the issues and Progress". You have a London broil… you ask for it to be well done (no red) when your waiter brings it to you, it looks browned & cooked until you open it, and it leaks blood. What would you have done to fix the problem? This is the same thing you will do to fix your inner problems. Fix the inner and the total meal will be more complete.

Imagine this: You have a London broil… you ask for it to be well done (no red) when your waiter brings it to you, it looks browned & cooked until you open it, and it leaks blood. What would you have done to fix the problem? This is the same thing you will do to fix your inner problems. Fix the inner and the total meal will be more complete. No introspection is equivalent to no progression.

Define confront.

_____

_____

_____

Why is it more important to address core issues rather than to focus on the surface?

_____

_____

_____

Your weaknesses give you a story to share with others. What are some of your weaknesses?

_____

_____

_____

The statement "Your story is not for you" is a quote that is often used. What does this statement mean to you?

_____

_____

_____

Why is it more important to address core issues rather than to focus on the surface?

_____

_____

_____

NOTES

RULE #15

RULE #15

THIS IS MY FREEDOM OF EXPRESSION. IT DOESN'T
MATTER WHAT I WEAR, IF THEY DON'T ACCEPT ME...
THAT'S THEIR FAULT.

RULE BREAKER

"Change your image, and change the people you attract."

Have you ever wanted to be the superstar who was ALWAYS chosen first for the game, but always got overlooked?

Was your image correct? Was your posture showing your confidence? Did you look like you were supposed to be playing, rather than being on the sideline? These are all the ways to project your image! Image is often the first thing people remember about you! What will you do to make sure that you look and act like a winner? Please understand: You do not have to focus on name brands, but rather neatness and the way you arrange your clothes and maintain your posture. While image is not everything, it is the "Thing" that will have you allow you to have doors opened for you in life. Remember, Like attracts like, and usually you are who you attract.

Define simulacrum.

_____

_____

_____

_____

Think about how you envision success. How does a successful person dress on a regular day?

_____

_____

_____

_____

If you wear a suit daily, would you want to be around a person who sags their pants or someone who dresses similar to you?

_____

_____

_____

_____

NOTES

69

RULE #16 ⟹

I CAN PUT EVERYTHING EXCEPT FOR
POSITIVITY IN MY HEAD, AND STILL MAINTAIN
A POSITIVE ATTITUDE!

RULE BREAKER

*"Life is like a farm, and you are
the gardener! Water your seeds with
wisdom and watch them grow to be
fruitful and plentiful!"*

When planning a successful garden, you must conduct research and chose what to feed your plants. If you fail to feed them the proper nutrients they will not grow. What will you feed your garden? Is there a negative environment in your garden that you are allowing to take the nutrients that are rightfully yours? If so, these weeds stunt your growth in life. They come in the form of friends and choices. Water your seeds with the proper guidance and knowledge, and many will admire your garden. When the work is plenty, so is the harvest. Admiration is a testament of your work.

Nationwide there exists a subculture of farming enthusiasts who travel nationwide to show off their prized crops. These farmers work throughout the year to produce the most hearty, tasty, abnormally sized and most colorful plants to present to expert judges. The rewards come in the form of money and the pride of their crops through their labor. Water and feed your garden right and reap huge rewards.

LINK TO LIFE EXERCISE

Define harvest.

_____

_____

_____

_____

If water, sunlight, soil, and air help plants to grow, what can help your dreams to grow and flourish?

_____

_____

_____

_____

Your friends represent the soil that you plant your seeds. What good characteristics do your friends possess in which will nourish your dreams?

_____

_____

_____

_____

In lawn and garden care, there are products that are designed to stop the growth of weeds, and that promote growth. What are the things that you can do to stop the "weeds" in your life? "Weeds" come in the form of friends, enemies and even family.

_____

_____

_____

_____

I AM YOUNG AND I HAVE A LONG LIFE TO LIVE.
I CAN BE RECKLESS NOW AND RESPONSIBLE
LATER IN MY LIFE.

RULE BREAKER

*"Treat life like your last dollar! Being
that you only have one, you can't
afford to waste any of it!"*

As Flava Flav would say… "DON'T believe the HYPE! DON'T… DON'T believe the HYPE"! The hype that we believe when we are younger is that we are invincible! We can't die and we have loads of time to waste and make mistakes! If you were on a game show, you would get the buzzer for being wrong with a mindset like that! Life is so fragile that you don't even know if you'll make it past the end of TODAY! So it is your responsibility to cherish the moments and get out and get something done! Not for anyone else, but rather yourself! Parents are NOT affected by your choices or decisions… YOU ARE! Let me share a scenario with you.

It was an extremely long week, and after bills, gas, and paying for his girlfriend Jasmine's hair to be done…Mike had 5 dollars left for one WHOLE day! He spent two on breakfast, two on lunch, and could not allow himself to spend that last dollar, in fear that he might need it for an emergency! Treat life like Mike's last dollar… don't waste it! If you thought of life in terms of money, you would treat each day as a more valuable aspect of life. Never take life for granted. Make sure you get the most out of it through being thankful, kindhearted, forgiving and living the fullest life that you can envision and safely experience.

Define cherish.

_____

_____

_____

_____

How do you feel when you're contemplating how to spend your last dollar?

_____

_____

_____

_____

Why is it so valuable to experience life as if it were your "last dollar"?

_____

_____

_____

_____

Do you currently live your life to your fullest potential? How can you improve?

_____

_____

_____

_____

NOTES

RULE #18

THE TEACHER IS BORING ME, SO I'M NOT
GOING TO ATTEMPT TO LEARN. NO INTEREST,
NO EFFORT.

RULE BREAKER

"Boredom is a self-inflicted disease that has side effects of underachievement, you have the cure!"

One thing that causes horrible effects on the body is boredom! An idle mind is not only the devil's playground, but also a victim of atrophy over time. In your everyday ventures, you must find inspiration in everything! There is good in each and everything you encounter. This is a skill that you will have to work on daily to strengthen your "Mental Muscles." Through gratification you will stimulate your mental capacity and train your brain to achieve more by default. With diligence, this is a feat at your grasp and will prove extremely valuable to becoming a high achiever. Defying the rules of boredom is solely your responsibility. Keep in mind that it is easy to be motivated by others, but the best motivation and inspiration is organic and gathered from within you.

 **LINK TO LIFE EXERCISE**

Define atrophy.

_____

_____

_____

_____

At the time of your boredom, what could have been an activity for you to complete rather than claiming to be bored?

_____

_____

_____

_____

What would have been a more effective action to take, and how would your results after you decided to take action, and not allow yourself to become bored?

_____

_____

_____

_____

Why does ambition atrophy with constant boredom?

_____

_____

_____

_____

RULE #19

I AM LIMITED TO MY SUCCESS AND
PRODUCTIVITY BECAUSE OF MY AGE. THERE
IS AN AGE LIMIT TO EVERYTHING!

RULE BREAKER

"Age is never a limitation once you pinpoint the proper angle of attack! NEVER LET YOUR AGE RANGE LIMIT YOUR PAY RANGE!"

Has anyone ever told you that you are too young, or too old to accomplish your dream? Throughout your life, it is inevitable that you will be told that statement many times! It is your responsibility to know that the person saying that is 10,000% false. Do not believe anyone who tells you this! You have something very unique that no other person possesses. Amongst many characteristics, beliefs, and values; it is your age! Due to your age you will ALWAYS possess a unique advantage! Find out what it is, and use it to your advantage! For Example: Do your grandparents possess the knowledge that you do about computers and pop culture? Of course they don't! Your age is never your weakness but rather your strength. FYI: If you want to increase your pay range, you must find three things. The three things you must find are a problem, a solution and who is going to pay for it. Now you have the formula to have your pay range increase! Thank me later…

Define ageism

_____
_____
_____
_____
_____

Write down the ways in which you have an advantage on your parents due to your age. (Computers, latest fashions, pop culture). All of these factors are advantages... now it's your responsibility to use them!

_____
_____
_____
_____
_____

What are examples of ageism in your community?

_____
_____
_____
_____
_____

How can you overcome ageisms?

_____
_____
_____
_____
_____

NOTES

RULE #20

I CAN ONLY GET ATTENTION WHEN I'M DOING
SOMETHING NEGATIVE.

RULE BREAKER

*"Controversy is the breeder of attention!
The question is: What are you going to
choose... Negative or Positive?"*

I LOVE CONTROVERSY!!!! The question is why? We are taught to believe that controversy is something to shy away from. Guns are also something we should stay away from, if we are not aware of how to use them! Controversy is your friend if you are trained on how to safely and effectively use it to your advantage! Controversy can cause you to be hated, imprisoned or the spotlight needed to create change in the world. It is your decision to decide whether it will be positive or negative. Do you feel as though there is too much violence in your city, not enough resources in your school, or way too many fights in school? Don't fight these problems with violence. Rather, use controversy to achieve your desired result! Create a group that shares your values, and make your concerns be heard. You have the power to overcome these issues and be victorious through solutions. Never be afraid of controversy. In the right hands, controversy will change the world in a monumental way.

What is controversy?

_____

_____

_____

_____

_____

How can you use controversy to help positively change your environment?

_____

_____

_____

_____

_____

What controversy has recently been in the media that has been used to positively affect people on a local or national level?

_____

_____

_____

_____

_____

NOTES

RULE #21

I DON'T HAVE TO MAKE PLANS FOR MY
SUCCESS. I JUST GO WITH THE FLOW.

RULE BREAKER

"Plans are NOT optional to successful people, and contrary to popular belief, without a plan… success is not an option."

Every project or great accomplishment has a beginning. What will your beginning be? Some have sight but lack vision. Even the smallest of tasks needs to have a vision associated with it to be fluid in making a tangible result and to become a finished product. While talking to my partner Kasan, we stumbled upon the topic of planning to achieve success. Kasan said something so basic, yet so essential. He stated; "Even when going to the bathroom, you must have a plan for your disposal to be successful." This was totally truth! Can you imagine going to the bathroom without planning to check for toilet paper before depositing into the bank of septic or not, planning to wipe/flush? Think about your successes and failures in life. I am willing to bet that you have more records of success accompanied with a solid plan. Plan now and have the winning record going forward!

Define prospective.

_____

_____

_____

_____

Plan out your morning routine thoroughly for a week, and then see how much more effective you are in accomplishing more tasks.

_____

_____

_____

_____

Write and record your personal plan for this next year. The plan does not have to be perfect, and will be changed as time goes along.

_____

_____

_____

_____

RULE #22

I HAVE NO CONTROL OVER THE OUTCOMES IN MY LIFE. I AM GOING TO DO WHAT IS CONSIDERED "SAFE." TAKING RISKS ARE TOO MUCH OF A THREAT TO MY SUCCESS.

RULE BREAKER

"If you are in a burning building, would you rather jump out of a window, or be burned? In life, when it feels like you are doomed, take chances or be consumed by the flames of mediocrity."

Having no control of your OUTCOME makes you loose control of your INCOME! The only safe I want to be bothered with is the SAFE that keeps my money secure!!! When you always wait for someone to "Give you some" you'll always end up the BROKE ONE!! Lets keep it real. No one likes being the person who needs help getting into the club!! We all have that friend that depends on others for their thrills and may even call you to help pay that sprint bill! When in reality, they have the key. Taking SMART risk is the key to be safe financially!

In life, we often times want to sit and wait for our rescue. This is not the way to reach the pinnacle of your success. There are endless possibilities for your life, but it is your responsibility to take advantage, pursue those possibilities and seize every day! While taking risks is key in success, one must focus on CALCULATED risk! This is risk with research and odds in your favor. Take a risk today! Scared money DOESN'T MAKE MONEY!

Define consummation.

_____

_____

_____

_____

Do you feel that it is better to be safe than sorry in achieving your dreams? Or are you more likely to be sorry through safety? Please explain your thoughts.

_____

_____

_____

_____

When have you succeeded by taking a risk?

_____

_____

_____

_____

NOTES

RULE #23

SUCCESS IS A QUICK COME-UP. I CAN RISE TO
THE TOP WITHOUT MUCH TROUBLE ON THE
WAY UP.

RULE BREAKER

*"When you are stressing on your
turbulence, remember that all planes
experience this feeling before they are
at a high enough altitude to cruise
through the clouds."*

Raise your hand if you have ever had trials and tribulations in your life. *Note to reader: People are going to look at you and question why you are raising your hand with no teacher in sight! Tell them Alfred E. Blake is your instructor. Now back to our scheduled message.* When your plane is in flight to the destination of success, there will be turbulence. There will be people who attempt to discourage you from your dreams and obstacles that you will have to overcome! Turbulence only occurs when you are in the process of achieving a higher altitude! You will NEVER face notable turbulence on the ground because the winds are not nearly as menacing at a low altitude! Turbulence means that you are headed in the right direction and that you are getting closer to your desired destination! Are you ready to embrace your turbulence?

LINK TO LIFE EXERCISE

Define turbulence.

_____

_____

_____

_____

_____

When you find that life gets tough for you, what are your methods to overcome?

_____

_____

_____

_____

_____

When you overcome your 'Turbulence' how do you feel?

_____

_____

_____

_____

_____

What are three examples of turbulence in your life?

_____

_____

_____

_____

NOTES

RULE #24

RIGHT NOW I NEED TO PUT MY ENERGY INTO
MY LOOKS, BECAUSE THAT IS THE MOST
IMPORTANT PART OF ME.

RULE BREAKER

*"I want you to realize that a nice
body and smile will wrinkle, and
fade over time! However, a beautiful
personality and character will only
grow over time."*

He or she might look delightful at first glance! BUT once you get a taste, that sourness will numb your taste buds to anything that moves talks or breathes like them! We tend to think MOST about the things that matter the LEAST! We have ALL done it! It is perfectly normal to be the bee that is attracted to the honey, it makes sense! If it looks good, you think its good! While it is possible, don't make outer beauty your FOCUS! Luckily for the bee, the pollen and honey have nutritional value and are beneficial to their health and essential to their survival. Somehow, the human species wasn't dealt that card when attraction comes into the picture!

You must make a pact today to look deeper than the surface! Have you ever looked at a delicious looking piece of fruit, and sliced it open to reveal rotten properties inside? When you focus solely on the surface, you neglect the inner rottenness that fruit may bear! Look for the core sweetness and the results will be much more fulfilling than looking for the shiny outer appearance. The sweetness of the core is the determining factor of nutrients received when you consume (People who surround you).

Define narcissist.

_____

_____

_____

_____

Compare the longevity of beauty to personality: which lasts longer? Is it more beneficial to invest in a long-term goal or a short-term goal? Explain.

_____

_____

_____

_____

Which would you invest more time into; fame or fortune? Out of the two, which has more longevity?

_____

_____

_____

_____

IN ORDER TO SCORE IN THE GAME OF LIFE, ALL
I NEED IS THE ANSWERS!

RULE BREAKER

"One of the biggest mistakes you can make in life is simply to look for the answer! Look for the Why's, What's, When's and How's!"

Hopefully you aren't a cheater and eye wanderer when it comes to a test! BUT if you have had wandering eyes you know that although you may have passed that test, you were unable to come up with the right answer without help! Have you ever had the case of being cross-eyed when you didn't know the answer on a test? I can't sit here and lie to you and say that I have never cheated on a test! I have! So be honest with yourself! I won't tell! While I made out for the moment, I lost big time for the long term! If that person were not there for the next test, the teacher would definitely know that a cheater was in the midst! When you cheat life's tests you cheat yourself! Look for those whys, what's and how's! Now to a personal and less incriminating story of mine:

As a child, I was the student that never wanted to complete division the long way! I always managed to find the answer by simply using my mental calculator. My teacher always deducted points from my assignments and I wondered why! Regardless of the method, I still had the correct answers! Now when I think about the situations, I realize why working and understanding the whole problem was necessary. In life, simply knowing the answer is not sufficient. You must search! Always find out the why, what, when, and how factor of every situation! Accept this concept and life will take on a new meaning, immediately! What's and why's allow you to arrive at your desired destination at will.

LINK TO LIFE EXERCISE

Define speculation.

_____

_____

_____

_____

_____

What is the current state of your life? Are you completely satisfied with your circumstances?

_____

_____

_____

_____

_____

If not, Why, when and how did you get to where you are now? How are you going to change your circumstances? If yes, how did you reach that point in your life? What choices were made to bring you to your current state?

_____

_____

_____

_____

_____

NOTES

RULE #26 ⟹

MY FRIENDS DON'T REPRESENT ME…
I AM MY OWN PERSON.

RULE BREAKER

"Would you wear a confederate flag, and claim not to be racist? So how can you spend time in the presence of bad company and claim to be good?"

If I were present you with a gift in the form of a Nazi flag, how would you feel about wearing it? You would undoubtedly feel uncomfortable not because of the design, but the meaning that is associated with the flag. You would feel weird because it is not an accurate representation of you! Most people would protest against wearing the flag because it doesn't stand for the things you believe in. I have a secret to share...

Your friends are your flag! The actions of the people you hang around or allow to hang around you are a representation of what you believe in. If your friends are representing great things, people will automatically assume the same is characteristic of you! When is the last time you have seen a homeless man hanging out with the Fortune 500 executives? My point exactly! You just don't see it! By no means am I saying that one person is better than the next, however, I want you to keep in mind that the flag you are flying with the company you keep. Most say guilty by association, I say successful by association! Today you must make the decision of what flag you will fly!

Define brand.

_____

_____

_____

_____

_____

They say you are the representation of the 5 people who you spend the most time with. Write those 5 people down and evaluate your relationship with them.

_____

_____

_____

_____

_____

Write down a specific list of things that you want to represent you and your personal brand.

_____

_____

_____

_____

_____

Is your company of acquaintances supplying you with resources to grow, and vice versa?

_____

_____

_____

_____

_____

NOTES

RULE #27 ⟶

ITS MY WAY OR NO WAY!

RULE BREAKER

"Elastic covers so much distance because of its ability to stretch! Be like elastic, and outstretch your hand, and ability to compromise…then watch your success grow!"

Are you an athlete? Better yet, have you ever played a sport or been involved in athletics? Great! Everyone can relate! We are made to stretch to prepare us for unexpected actions during activity! Stretching represents compromise, and activity represents your life! You must learn to compromise in life, and "stretch" daily! Do you want to live a less stressful life? Do you want to produce more success in life? Learn to be ELASTIC!! Elastic covers more ground in its natural state than steel... EVERY DAY! Being able to stretch is being able to adapt to change. Life is all about adaptation; natural selection (Darwin) applies to you also!

Define irrepressible.

_____

_____

_____

_____

Does compromise make you more or less likely to achieve personal success? Share your reason for why or why not.

_____

_____

_____

_____

How can you compromise to help move forward in your life today? Name 5 ways.

_____

_____

_____

_____

117

RULE #28

I MUST GRIND TO MAKE IT!
(WORK SMARTER, NOT HARDER.)

RULE BREAKER

"Grinding daily will be abrasive and damaging to your engine. Use oil, and allow your gears to shift smoothly until you succeed, and glide!"

Stop saying I'm on my grind! What is a grind? Grinding is described as an abrasive rubbing of multiple surfaces and crushing! So, with that being said why would you claim "Being on the daily grind"? You must dedicate your life to find your individual "Glide"! This is meant to have you think and make the promise to work smarter, and not harder! Think about how effortlessly an air hockey puck glides across the board. Wouldn't you like to sail effortlessly from where you are to your goal? Find out how to focus your energy into channels that will allow you to "glide" to the top!

Define abrasive.

_____

_____

_____

_____

Would you rather endure less hardship or more on the journey to your ultimate success?

_____

_____

_____

_____

Identify an activity that you have been involved in, where working smarter will help you get ahead of your competition! How can you "glide" to reach your destination in a more smooth natutre?

_____

_____

_____

_____

Visualization: If given the choice, would you rather move like an air hockey puck, or an uneven rock when moving closer to success?

_____

_____

_____

_____

RULE #29 →

"WHAT'S IN FASHION IN THE NEWS IS HOW I
SHOULD DRESS!"

RULE BREAKER

*"Do you want to be a Las Vegas act or
the inspiration for the Las Vegas act?
Being unique is the key to the latter.
Being a copycat is the key to the first!"*

Have you ever heard of the Burmese ruby? This is the most precious gem known to man! Would you believe me if I told you that you possess more value than that gem? Most likely, you would say where the heck is it, and when can I cash in! Luckily for you, I have the answer to both questions. The gem is inside your originality as a human being with unlimited possibility. You will cash in once you use this personal equation that I am sharing with you. Talent + Skills + Service = Purpose $(T+S+S=P)$. Accept your purpose, and reap priceless rewards! Why be a cubic zirconium when you harvest more value than the most valuable gem on earth? Most people claim not to know how to find their purpose in life. You no longer can utter those words!

Define facsimile.

_____
_____
_____
_____

Identify your trademark quality. In other words, what is your most effective skill or quality that you are known for?

_____
_____
_____
_____
_____

How does your trademark quality distinguish you from your peers?

_____
_____
_____
_____
_____

Talent + Skill + Service = Purpose
What is your talent, skill, and service to others?

_____
_____
_____
_____

RULE #30

WHAT FORMULA WORKS FOR OTHERS,
WILL WORK FOR ME!

RULE BREAKER

"Life is like a recipe, continue to try different ingredients until YOU have the perfect consistency."

You are not meant to reach success on your first try! If life and achieving the things you dreamt about were that simple, we would have no desire to accomplish these feats! It is your responsibility to design your own unique recipe for success. You must not try one time; you have to dedicate time and effort to constantly and continuously improve your prepared meal. The key to the proper recipe is to prepare according to your taste buds (What works best for you). Make improvements on your recipe daily until your consistency, flavor, and texture are to your liking! Remember, you will have to season according to your desired flavor!

Define concoction.

_____

_____

_____

_____

What are three ways in which your texture/flavor are judged in life?

_____

_____

_____

_____

How can you get closer to making your recipe great?

_____

_____

_____

_____

Find 3 books that interest you, and highlight 3 life strategies from each, and customize them to fit your life.

_____

_____

_____

_____

I CAN'T HELP BEING UPSET, AND ACTING ON MY
EMOTIONS. MY EMOTIONS MAKE ME WHO I AM.

RULE BREAKER

"The average person is ruled by emotions, the successful person is ruled by logic!"

When is the last time you said to a friend, "I love instability and being controlled by unstable people!" I already know your answer. This is the first time you've heard this and the last, unless you plan on reading that statement repeatedly! One thing you are designed to crave is stability! If we don't have stability we start to undergo signs of uncertainty and begin to breakdown. Emotions are not to be ruling factors, therefore don't use them for the incorrect purpose! Use logic and excel more than others around you! You may ask why logic is the ruler of the two. Emotions force you to act responsively rather than intuitively, and with reason. Ask prisoners whether they acted with emotion or through thinking things through completely. This should help to solidify your mindset! Use logic and levitate! I'm waiting for you at the top!

Define logic.

_____
_____
_____
_____
_____

Identify a situation where you acted out of emotion.

_____
_____
_____
_____
_____

List how you could have acted differently by allowing logic to supersede emotion.

_____
_____
_____
_____
_____

What is the difference in the two outcomes?

_____
_____
_____
_____

NOTES

RULE #32

YOU DON'T HAVE TO WORRY ABOUT MY ATTITUDE I'M
GOOD! I KNOW I HAVE A BAD ATTITUDE AND I AM NOT
AFFECTED...I'M STILL GOING TO BE SUCCESSFUL.

RULE BREAKER

*"Attitude is similar to a plane ride.
Your view is limited when you start.
When the altitude of your attitude
increases, the more territory is open for
your eyes to envision."*

As a youth, my attitude was me, me, me, and I, I, I. That attitude continually led me down the path to failure! Keep your attitude focused on positivity and how you can help your fellow brother/sister and watch your surroundings transform before your eyes! I challenge you to take a look at your classmates and their attitudes. Observe what opportunities are available to the students who have positive attitudes in comparison to those with negative ones. The differences will be like night and day. The question is which would you like to experience? Once you whole-heartedly make the decision to change your attitude, your life has no choice but to morph as well.

LINK TO LIFE EXERCISE

Define altitude.

_____

_____

_____

_____

_____

Envision a plane ride... How is altitude used metaphorically to show differences in attitude?

_____

_____

_____

_____

What commitment will you make to yourself to increase the altitude of your attitude?

_____

_____

_____

_____

How do you think your life will change once you apply a change of attitude?

_____

_____

_____

_____

What difference can your attitude make amongst your friends?

_____

_____

_____

_____

RULE #33 $\longrightarrow$

COMPLAIN AND FEEL BETTER ABOUT YOUR MISHAPS
AND PROBLEMS IN LIFE!

RULE BREAKER

"People who complain about what is not happening for them are the ones who don't appreciate what is."

There is always something to be thankful for! As human beings, we innately yearn for more than we have. While you are looking for that extra couple dollars or more fortune, you are missing the things that you are blessed to have. As you read this message, I want you to pause and think of five things to be thankful for. Off the top of my dome, I know at least five things that you are to be grateful for.

- Since you are reading this, you are alive!
- You have the ability see these words (Brail version hasn't been released yet) we know you have the gift of sight.
- You have had the chance to have a decent enough education to be able to read and comprehend.
- You have the mindset that many people don't have... you are reading this book to improve your life, and the people's lives around you due to your change.
- You have the absolute panacea to your problems in this book!

Remember this... no matter what you are experiencing keep your head up, and always be grateful! When you appreciate what you have, more is given to you.

Define panacea.

_____

_____

_____

_____

Observe your surroundings this week, and write down all the disadvantages that you see everyone around you facing.

_____

_____

_____

_____

Write down 5 possessions that you are blessed to have.

_____

_____

_____

_____

I CAN EXCEL BY LEARNING ABOUT EVERYTHING BUT MYSELF. I HAVE NO NEED TO LEARN MYSELF MORE IN-DEPTH.

RULE BREAKER

"Realization of self is the most powerful realization possible! How can you properly maneuver a vehicle without knowing what makes it go?"

How valuable is a car/bicycle before learning how to use it? Take a second to think back to when you first got that bike that you'd always wanted. In reality, the only thing the bike was useful for was bringing you closer to getting another scar on your body! In essence it was USELESS until you knew how it operated and how you could use it to your advantage! You must introspectively view yourself, and how you function! In conclusion, if you want to arrive at your goal, you must familiarize yourself with your vehicle. Start riding, and embrace falling off today! These lessons, failures and successes will mold you to become the best at being you!

Define maneuver.

_____
_____
_____
_____

What type of gas (Motivation, Inspiration, etc.) do you need to function?

_____
_____
_____
_____

What motivates you, and what makes you tick, and excited to excel?

_____
_____
_____
_____

NOTES

RULE #35

I HAVE THE RAW TALENT THAT NO ONE ELSE
HAS, I HAVE IT MADE! I JUST HAVE TO SHOW UP…
DEVELOPMENT ISN'T NEEDED.

RULE BREAKER

*"The secret to winning is development!
You already have what is needed
to win!"*

Standing at 370 feet tall, weighing in at 1.6 million pounds, this mutant of an organism started as a seed; a seed the size of a tomato plant. Despite the seed's minute stature, this organism has grown to be massive through development! This is the fundamental difference between success and failure. What you begin with has no direct effect on what you work to achieve! So no matter the talent that you naturally possess, you must be aware of the importance of development! You have the ability to be larger than life, but you must first earmark time daily to hone your skills. When you apply techniques that better you as a person, you can then hypothetically grow to exceed the size of the legendary giant redwood tree.

Define matriculate.

_____

_____

_____

_____

Research how three people in history have overcome adversity in order to achieve their missions (I have four in mind: Thomas S. Monaghan, Ben Carson, Richard Branson and Michael Jordan.).

_____

_____

_____

_____

How do their struggles compare to yours in magnitude?

_____

_____

_____

_____

List 3 similarities and differences.

_____

_____

_____

_____

149

RULE #36

WHEN PREVENTABLE TRAGEDIES OCCUR, I JUST
DUST MY SHOULDERS OFF AND KEEP IT MOVING.
I JUST HAD BAD LUCK, I CAN ACT THE WAY I DID
BEFORE, AND NOT WORRY ABOUT IT HAPPENING
AGAIN.

RULE BREAKER

*"Sometimes it takes a horrible crash to
realize that your vehicle needs repairs!
Don't crash your life in order to learn
that lesson…open your eyes!"*

Have you changed your oil lately? There are so many things that you should know when you jump into the seat of your first car. They include knowing how to change windshield wipers, how and when to put air in your tires and more importantly when to change your oil! When you get your car, the one thing that most people are told is that they MUST change their oil every 3000 miles! If you don't, PLEASE DO NOT be surprised if your check engine light comes on and if ignored, you end up on the side of the road in the freezing cold with your thumb out begging for help or worst your engines ceases and you end up in a car accident. The engine is the core of your vehicle. Your personal core represents your emotional, mental, physical, and social health. Earlier I mentioned your "Check Engine" light.

Are you familiar with the check engine light in a car? This light informs the driver of service needed. Bad grades, constant altercations with people, your clothes don't fit anymore? These are all indicators that your check engine light is on and you that you need fixing! I remember the first time I realized I needed to lose weight. As I went up the eighth flight of stairs I nearly passed out! How many times have we been notified of a repair needed, and failed to acknowledge it? By not acknowledging, we increase the possibility to crash into depression, disease and lack of desired results. Ignore needed repairs, and you risk crashing and totaling your life. There are signs of repair that surround us in life. If we decide not to acknowledge them, we decide to fail in life.

Define catastrophes.

_____

_____

_____

_____

Think about a time when you made a huge mistake, and had to deal with the repercussions. Describe that mistake and repercussions.

_____

_____

_____

_____

What will you do next time to change the outcome?

_____

_____

_____

_____

WHEN PEOPLE WHO ARE NOT MOVING TOWARD
SUCCESS SURROUND ME, I ALLOW THEM TO STAY
AROUND, AND TOLERATE THEM.

RULE BREAKER

"A scorpion is only deadly to those in close proximity!"

What is a scorpion? A scorpion is a deadly arachnid that has the power to bring a 300 pound man to their death through a simple pinch. Often time's youth and adults alike are "pinched" by the people they allow to surround them. In your life a scorpion can take the form of disgruntled family members, wayward and unmotivated friends, drugs, and other things that will poison. It is your responsibility to realize you have the control to remove these scorpions' from your environment. You simply disassociate yourself by moving as far away from them as you can. I have removed scorpions from my life and you can too. If you allow scorpions to loiter in your midst, you risk your dreams being poisoned by their wrath.

Define loiter.

_____

_____

_____

_____

How can friends who aimlessly wander through life help you to succeed?

_____

_____

_____

_____

Research the warning signs that a scorpion gives when they are about to attack?

_____

_____

_____

_____

How are their similar to warning signs in a friendship/relationship?

_____

_____

_____

_____

RULE #38 $\longrightarrow$

MY CIRCUMSTANCES, AND THE ENVIRONMENT THAT
I GREW UP IN WILL DETERMINE WHERE I END UP IN
MY CAREER/LIFE. I AM LIMITED BECAUSE OF THE
ENVIRONMENTAL FACTORS THAT SURROUND ME.

RULE BREAKER

*"Find it, cherish it, take it out, polish
it, and then place it on display for
others to admire!" "Diamond in the
rough mentality"*

As I sit here and listen to Trey Songz and Drake's song "Successful"… I recite the words that we all utter to ourselves at one point in life. "I just want to be successful" is a statement that serves as everyone's dream! Growing up in East Orange, N.J. I was in a war-filled zone until my mother decided to move to the suburbs. There were many others who weren't as lucky as me! They are in the "Cave" known as the hood. Inside that cave there are millions of undiscovered diamonds. You are a precious gem! The question is: Do you believe me? Now, it is your duty to excavate your inner qualities and talents and cherish them. Once you find your "Diamonds" you must let others see them, add polish and let others see your luster. Afterwards, pay it forward by giving someone hope from your success.

Define excavate.

_____

_____

_____

_____

Name three ways that you can ultimately become closer to becoming the diamond you want to share worldwide.

_____

_____

_____

_____

Record how your environment (parents, community, etc.) have shaped and molded you in a positive way.

_____

_____

_____

_____

NOTES

RULE #39

I HAVE FAILED MANY TIMES IN ACHIEVING MY DREAMS.
I MAY NEED TO STOP OR SLOW DOWN WITH MY VISION.

RULE BREAKER

"You must run like a fugitive towards your goal! If you stop, you become imprisoned to mediocrity."

Mediocrity is the archenemy of success. Mediocrity goes against everything that success stands for. As a progressive individual it is essential that you realize that raising your standards isn't optional… it is the rule of the game of success. Visualize a prisoner who has just escaped from prison. He is being pursued by multiple agencies that have the same goal of capturing him, and never letting him free again. What happens if he stops? He gets caught, and is back to being imprisoned with no chance of getting away from his harsh reality. The same is true for you in your pilgrimage towards success. So, next time you think of stopping, think of the visualization I just shared with you. You are not to stop or look back. Run until you have achieved your goals!

Define pilgrimage.

_____

_____

_____

_____

If you were a fugitive what would make your escape successful
(planning, research, action, etc...) be specific.

_____

_____

_____

_____

Many musicians and icons in pop culture can be put into the category of fugitives to
mediocrity. Name 2 and briefly share a piece of their stories.

_____

_____

_____

_____

RULE #40 ⟹

I NEED ATTENTION IF I WANT TO BE SOMETHING.
EVERYONE WHO IS SOMEONE IS THAT PERSON
BECAUSE OF ATTENTION.

RULE BREAKER

"Longing for attention is the reason for most people's actions. Being addicted to attention is the most dangerous narcotic available to human kind."

You may ask why attention is dangerous. In reality, there is absolutely nothing wrong with attention. It is the need for attention that is dangerous and detrimental to your health. Attention is a by-product of something noteworthy and substantial. You have the responsibility to aim for noteworthy accomplishments. However, your passion and the reason you complete your accomplishments need to be rooted in a deeper and bigger purpose than solely gaining acclaim. You cannot make attention your overall goal, but rather something that comes along with your work. An "at any cost attitude" is an expensive habit/attitude to possess. Whatever you do, keep your morals and stay focused on your mission and NOT ATTENTION!

Define necessitous.

_____

_____

_____

_____

_____

Why is it a disadvantage to be necessitous in life?

_____

_____

_____

_____

_____

What are two examples of people who have fell victim of losing fame?

_____

_____

_____

_____

_____

In your opinion, do you think the loss of fame was their downfall? Why?

_____

_____

_____

_____

_____

THE MORE PEOPLE KNOW WHOM I ASSOCIATE
WITH, THE MORE THEY RESPECT ME FOR MY
STATUS.

RULE BREAKER

*"The easiest way to become a sitting
duck is to disclose all your relationships
with random people and associates."*

Do you remember the game DUCK DUCK...GOOSE? DON'T LIE!!! You know you used to beg to play Duck Duck Goose during free time!!! As a teacher, I love when students ask to play!!! Its HILLARIOUS to watch kids running around a circle and all the "involuntary tumbles" that happen in between. When you disclose your closest relationships, you become a sitting duck/goose with no defense or idea when you will be "goosed"! If you were given a choice to be any creature in the animal kingdom, out of all the animals I have serious doubts that you'd want to become a goose so don't start now.

Why would you set yourself up for failure purposely? Once others get to know your relationships with people, they know how to reach you and your targets. Knowledge is power! The question is, how much knowledge are you willing to give to someone who is unauthorized to handle it properly? Once you allow that much insight into your life, you allow wayward minds to strategically capitalize on it. Don't allow people to have leverage over you unnecessarily. The privilege of one knowing your relationships can make or break you... depending on whose hands this information is in. Share cautiously.

Define unveil.

What factors are important to establish trust when unveiling your personal relationships?

Imagine you know someone and want to affect him or her in a negative way. They have two friends that they hang with, but don't know about the issue you have with them. Who is now a target to get to them? How can you get to your intended target through their friends?

RULE #42

I ACT UNINTERESTED IN SCHOOL BECAUSE I
DON'T CARE HOW I FINISH MY HIGH SCHOOL
CAREER.

RULE BREAKER

"In life we all want a winning a medal! Not one of us wants to merely be in the game."

Think about the last competition you competed in. Upon entry, what was your goal? If you are like most people, you wanted to WIN! Everyone wants to win! The question is, what are you willing to do to distinguish yourself from the rest? If everyone else is a cloud, you must shoot to be a star. If all others are aiming to be stars, you must aim to be a constellation of stars! Always aim to do bigger and better. This is what winners have stored in their minds. Do not confuse the message, winners are not under the impression that they area better than others, but rather working towards being able to be the best. Whether or not you win, is the least valuable in any competition. The drive to strive for the top is the separating factor of those who excel and those who just participate.

Define victor.

_____

_____

_____

_____

What feelings do you have when heading into a competition? Do you want to win, lose, or feel indifferent? What are the reasons for your respective feelings?

_____

_____

_____

_____

What must you do differently to excel more than your competitors? How much more time, effort, and research do you need to come out on top?

_____

_____

_____

_____

FAST LIFE AND FAST MONEY IS THE WAY TO
ENJOY LIFE THE MOST!

RULE BREAKER

*"Cook life like a trained chef. Take
things slow, and allow them to
marinate for a more robust flavor!"*

If given the choice, would you prefer a succulent slow-cooked Honey BBQ burger, seasoned perfectly with oregano and topped with your favorite cheese or a McDonalds cheeseburger? Now lets think about life and the direct connection between how food is prepared and how you operate in life! Society has made most things that we desire easy to attain. Due to this you have been under the impression that you are to receive what you desire when you want it. What I just described is called immediate gratification. We often rush life and want the robust flavor that you cannot get out of a quickly prepared meal! I challenge you to take your time, and marinate your habits, goals and business attitude! Let's live life like trained chefs! Take your time and enjoy your robust flavor that comes as a result of your preparation!

Define marinate.

_____

_____

_____

_____

If marinate means to submerge and allow flavors to seep into the core, how can you relate marinating meat to your life?

_____

_____

_____

_____

What types of people, habits, and actions will you immerse yourself in to extract a savory life?

_____

_____

_____

_____

IF I WAIT LONG ENOUGH FOR MY TIME TO COME,
SOMEONE WILL EVENTUALLY GIVE ME MY BIG BREAK
AND TAKE ME TO THE TOP!

RULE BREAKER

"Dismiss the goldfish mentality! Don't wait for someone to feed you and take care of you! Go out and get your own!"

Do you remember the first animal that you asked for as a child? If not, dig deep into your memory and think about what animal you were deprived of. Not getting the animal you wanted as a child should be considered a universal rites of passage when it comes to becoming an adolescent. Everyone and their momma was told no about one of those pets that would absolutely turn you into the best and most responsible super child...if they would have gotten it for you! I know a slew of girls who wanted a real "Pony" and got the doll, the boys who wanted the snake and got a worm or the people who wanted a dog and got NOTHING!

If you've never had the dog, cat, iguana, whale, or lion you always wanted, you probably had that void filled by a goldfish! They are low-maintenance, easily replaceable and easy to forget! While they are cute, and easy to maintain, stay away from them! You must do everything in your power to separate yourself from the mindset of a goldfish! In life, there are always individuals who claim to be helpless, and cannot fend for themselves. You are not helpless! If you decide and make the commitment to excel, you will! Stop waiting for the food to come to you! Get up and get it!

Define delve.

_____

_____

_____

_____

There are tons of resources available to you. Which should you delve into daily to bring you closer to success?

_____

_____

_____

_____

How can you act on your dream today? What is your first action to stop being dependent on others?

_____

_____

_____

_____

Would you rather live life like a shark or goldfish? Why?

_____

_____

_____

_____

THE OUTER APPEARANCE IS WHAT IS MOST
VALUABLE, AND WILL DETERMINE MY VALUE
TO OTHERS.

RULE BREAKER

*"Many people are rich on the outside
in order to cover for the recession on
the inside! Figure which one you are
today, and act accordingly."*

New Mercedes Benz, closets filled to the brim with shoes in crisp boxes, jewelry for each day of the month… all with no added value to self. These are the symptoms that many suffer from daily. Often people feel that they are less valuable in life if they do not possess material things. This state of mind takes place due to the images that are displayed in the media. These images are said to be the valuable assets in life but in reality, they are mere accessories. The true value is found in your heart, your action, and what difference you make in the lives of others. "What good is it for a man to profit the entire world, and lose their soul?" Many people get rich on the outside, as a replacement for the inner emptiness. The journey to recession proofing yourself is a process that can be achieved regardless of what's going on in our economy, and it starts with developing internally. While there is nothing wrong with attaining material possessions, you inner qualities will allow you to sustain them.

Define façade.

_____

_____

_____

_____

Take an inventory of your most valued possessions. Evaluate whether these possessions make you who you are, or act as accessories.

_____

_____

_____

_____

What is it that makes people gravitate towards you? If their reasons are materialistic, do you really want these people around you?

_____

_____

_____

_____

NOTES

RULE #46

I LISTEN TO NO ONE, BECAUSE I KNOW
MOSTLY ALL I NEED TO KNOW.

RULE BREAKER

"Knowing too much to listen, is a sign of not knowing at all."

One of the most harmful phrases known to man is " I already know that". You may think that knowing a lot of information about something is a sign of enlightenment. While it is a blessing to be informed about a myriad of things, many people allow perceived knowledge to stop them from excelling. Always keep in mind: information has no plateau! You always have room to be enlightened and increase your storage capacity of facts. While you may have some knowledge, always be open to hear others opinion and angles on topics and issues; always be open to new knowledge. When you allow yourself to believe that you are omniscient, you decide to stop any new knowledge from being attained. Failure to accept new wisdom and facts means that you have stopped growing. This is the worst point that you can reach in life. Always be ready to learn and add to the CPU of your brain, and expand the sponge in your head with useful information.

Define plateau.

_____

_____

_____

_____

What is the disadvantage in thinking that you have reached your plateau?

_____

_____

_____

_____

Think of your hobbies, go online and Google ways to improve your skills, and attempt others methods all week.

_____

_____

_____

_____

List how you have helped others with improving their skills.

_____

_____

_____

_____

I DON'T HAVE TO WORRY ABOUT SHORT-TERM
GOALS. I AM GOING FOR THE BIG SCORE.

RULE BREAKER

*"Life is like a football game, it's
difficult to win with only Hail Mary's
(Football)… running the ball for short
goals help set you up for the big score
and both are necessary to win."*

While speaking to a good friend and successful businessman in Atlanta, we discussed the importance of long and short-term goals. He has a profound way of looking at life. He stated something in an analytical sense to baseball:

"Don't always focus on the home run… it's the single hitters that make the most impact." Don't solely shoot for the major feats, and forget the minor aspects. Homerun hitters have lower batting percentages, and are usually good for that one thing…. Be versatile in your approach to the game of success! - Ahmad Jamal (CEO of Billionaire Nation Wealth Brand Management & Mktg)

Through this statement you are able to keep in mind that short-term goals are just as important as long-term goals. Each type of goal setting is essential to the success of the other. Life is about spreading your goals, and efforts equally. If the opportunity for the home run comes, take it, but don't rely on it! A base or double hit is better than a no-hitter!

Define prioritize.

_____

_____

_____

_____

_____

What is your ultimate goal for the next 3 years? Break this goal down into short–term and long-term goals. A three-month increment will serve as the appropriate model.

_____

_____

_____

_____

_____

Also, list some of the challenges you may face along the way.

_____

_____

_____

_____

_____

How will you approach those challenges?

_____

_____

_____

_____

_____

NOTES

RULE #48

I DON'T HAVE TO FORGIVE MY PARENTS FOR HOW
THEY HAVE NEGATIVELY AFFECTED MY LIFE. THEY
MADE THEIR NEGATIVE IMPACT, AND THAT CAN
NEVER BE CHANGED.

RULE BREAKER

*"Learn to forgive your parents, for
their mistakes that have negatively
affected your life; or never forgive
yourself for the people and
things you lose as a result of your
unforgiving spirit."*

We have heard and recited the phrase "Learn to forgive and forget" numerous times in our lives! However, few will actually explain why or how this will benefit you in life. Let me assist you. When you hold in negative feelings and emotions, you halt progress indefinitely. Adverse feelings towards parents are associated with all parent/child relationships! There is no relationship that does not have its problems. Parents only do what they know to do. Practices they engage in are inherited from their parental guidance or lack thereof. You may peel an orange, and eat it and I may cut it in half, and scoop out the inner goodness! We have different approaches to get to the center, but we have the same vision in mind. Even if your parents were not in your life, and have caused much hurt and anxiety in your life... Once you forgive, you find peace. Remember, "Release = Relief!"

Define redemption.

_____

_____

_____

_____

Go home today and try talking with your parent/s about how you have been
adversely affected by their parenting. Hear their side of the story, and allow
yourself to forgive them.

_____

_____

_____

_____

Record what you learned and how you will do differently when you become a parent.

_____

_____

_____

_____

RULE #49

I AM FROM A DYSFUNCTIONAL FAMILY, SO I DON'T
HAVE THE OPPORTUNITY TO SUCCEED AS OTHERS
WITH A FUNCTIONAL FAMILY. I AM FROM AN
AFFLUENT BACKGROUND, SO I CANNOT RELATE TO
OTHERS OF LOWER SOCIO-ECONOMIC STATUS.

RULE BREAKER

"Never let your reality be your excuse!"

I'm poor, and I will never be the same place in life with the affluent. I just don't possess the skills and know-how to operate in their presence. This is the statement that came out of a student's mouth. When Ralph said this, my heart dropped. Not because he was misinformed, but because there are millions who actually have that misconception. Although we come from different places and have different experiences, they all make us stronger as individuals, and ultimately as a community. Your current reality is not a permanent situation. It is totally up to you to change your reality. It is your responsibility to use the situations you hate the most to chase what you love the most! Your reality is your strong point. It will shape your thoughts, strengths, and weaknesses. Overall, it makes you unique and able to tackle situations that others can never fathom. Embrace your reality. Through embracing my reality, you are able to read this book today!

Define misconception.

_____

_____

_____

_____

List five ways that your reality both negative and positive; is strengthened by your circumstances.

_____

_____

_____

_____

How are you going to make your reality work towards your success? How is your reality your advantage?

_____

_____

_____

_____

NOTES

RULE #50

I LOOK OUT FOR OTHERS FIRST, AND THEN I HELP
MYSELF AFTERWARDS.

RULE BREAKER

*"What others do for you is a
directly proportional to what you
do for yourself."*

Always remember, what people do for you, is a direct measure of what you do for yourself. If you are a model, you work out, spend hours in the gym, and fight yourself to fight the urges of JUNK FOOD! Your rewards are the fact that people compliment you on your body! You are able to use your body to make money, and acquire other things! If you are an artist, you don't get a record deal for just making a hot SINGLE! You get a deal from creating a buzz and a following! Once again, you have done that for yourself first, and now people do not MIND GIVING their time and money to help you! However, this only COMES WHEN YOU HELP YOURSELF OUT! No one wants to help someone who doesn't help themselves! That is why many of you reading will see a person who is always begging for money at the same place! They are relying on someone else doing for him or her without helping themselves first!

Define proportional.

_____
_____
_____
_____
_____

How are jobs and careers proportional to amount of education pursued?
(Ex. Nurse, Lawyer, Teacher, Entrepreneur.)

_____
_____
_____
_____
_____

Ponder on how students are rewarded for doing well for themselves academically throughout and post high school. Would you rather help a someone who is slacker or hard worker? Why?

_____
_____
_____
_____
_____

I HAVE FORGOTTEN MY PAST BECAUSE IT'S NO
LONGER MY REALITY.

RULE BREAKER

*"Forgetting where you come from
is the way to find yourself back
where you started."*

The journey to the top is a long road, and once the car begins to drive on cruise control, we tend to forget how we got there! Humility is something that is preached and you must adhere to it, or lose what you have gained or are destined to gain! Never forget where you came from, and always reach down and help someone! That's what my team and I do, and have been successful thus far! Lets continue this and make the world how we want it! Next time you talk about someone being a certain way, I want you to inspect your behavior, and make sure that you are acting the right way!

A great man once said that the successfulness of your business endeavors is dependant on upon your ability to leverage relationships!! Learn how to treat people! We need each other to thrive! Lets not forget it!

Define abjure.

_____
_____
_____
_____
_____

Challenge yourself to remember the feelings that you had before you succeeded at whatever task you have overcome. Write down the feelings you had before taking a very important test in your academic career, or sports game you had to win to have your name embedded in history. Vow to never forget the feeling and this will keep you at the top of your game.

_____
_____
_____
_____
_____

Do you believe that forgetting where you came from is counterproductive in reaching success? Why or why not?

_____
_____
_____
_____
_____

NOTES

RULE #52

ALTHOUGH MY FRIENDS ARE NOT TAKING ACTION
TO BE SUCCESSFUL, I MUST STICK BY THEM. IF I
DON'T, I AM A TRAITOR.

RULE BREAKER

*"Leaving unmotivated friends is
never a betrayal of the friend…
but staying IS a betrayal of
yourself, and your NIRVANA."*

Throughout life, we are programmed to have a bigger fear of betraying others rather than the thought of doing a disservice to ourselves. Lets get elementary on this topic. When you were in pre-school, you were taught to treat everyone nice, and that all people were equally deserving of your friendship. Unfortunately when pre-school kids become adolescents, we still have those learned behaviors programmed in our psyche. You have remnants of that lesson which serves as a disadvantage to your livelihood if not addressed. If there are friends in your circle that are not aiming towards success, you must upgrade them! Don't be misconstrued; you should attempt to inform them of making more fruitful choices in life, but don't lose out on your blessings due to your association with unmotivated friends and the fruit or lack thereof from their labor.

Define nirvana.

_____
_____
_____
_____
_____

How can your association of friends bring you closer to or further from nirvana?

_____
_____
_____
_____
_____

A popular statement is "Guilty by association". How will you challenge yourself to change that to successful by association.

_____
_____
_____
_____
_____

APPLY THESE RULES TO LIFE

POST-WORD

I met Alfred Blake in the spring of 2008 at an empowerment conference for young men. From the very first meeting I knew this young man had sheer determination, desire and the fortitude to be a life-changer. Alfred has always been about action rather than rhetoric. When he told me that he was going to author a book, I had no doubt that he would. I have had the opportunity and privilege to mentor Alfred and I have learned so much from him on the meaning and expectations on being a mentee. I too have mentors and Alfred has shown me with his actions on how I can become a better mentee myself. Alfred has a very bright future and I am looking forward to seeing it unfold.

This book, Breaking All the Rules, will lay a solid foundation for all that read it. Alfred does a great job of providing the reader with concepts as well as exercises that will provide thought provoking actions leading to next level personal development. I am looking forward to seeing the lives that are changed by those who dare to be different as they learn how to Break All The Rules...The Right Way.

–Alvin S. Perry

ACKNOWLEDGMENTS

This book is dedicated to all who have failed and made a decision that their current state at the time was NOT their final state. This is for all the students who have been deemed hopeless and set out to make those statements a fallacy.

I would like to thank my mother; her stern nature and caring spirit have nurtured my rebellious soul, and helped to turn my rebellion into epiphany. Her faith in me when I disappointed her time after time is not forgotten. One thing that I will always carry that was instilled from a young man is the affirmation… "I am a genius if I apply my knowledge." That phrase was helpful in helping me become aware of my nature as a genius.

I would like to thank my father for the example that he has set as a wise man of standard and principle. Through my father's guidance, I have been able to develop a sense of pride without being boastful, strength through hard work without being overbearing… and the essence of strong will with a purpose. I have learned to greet people from all walks of life with the same respect and smile. I gained my peaceful fortitude from him.

I would like to thank my best friend Myke "Drink" Grubbs for his constant support and frank advice regardless of the response I wanted to hear. I appreciate the comfort on the days when I felt as though I wouldn't make it. More than anything, I am thankful for the unconditional love we share and the brotherhood that we have developed, despite not sharing parents. Thanks for being that voice when no one else understood or wanted to be truthful.

I would like to thank Kasan Lane… You are the creative genius that the world will soon come to acknowledge. I am grateful for being able to share the space of a dreamer with you. We have covered more miles than the state of NJ traveling and making our goals and dreams become a reality. We have been everywhere from man hunting Kanye West in Manhattan to working with Pharrell Williams to empower youth and being "Bamboozled" out of money on several occasions.

I would like to thank Mr. Alvin Perry for helping to shave my learning curve as a speaker and entrepreneur. While there were others who I asked, most spoke with no action. You have allowed me to grow tremendously, and through your counsel "I keep my feet moving" because I am always one step away from positive change.

To my family: Grandma thanks for always bringing a smile to my face through your stories and wise advice. Aunt Debbie thanks for always giving me a place to escape to, and helping me with my endeavors in the kitchen. Uncle Al thanks for punching me in the chest when I was deserving of it, and for not letting me quit Pop-Warner. Through your actions I learned a valuable lesson that has helped me throughout life. Thanks to Aunt Barb for being present to give encouragement when others doubted and thank you for always being eager to share a laugh.

Thanks to Justified communications LLC and Mrs. Shears for the deft editing of The Students Handbook To Breaking All The Rules. I would also like to thank Mrs. Shears for always being a supporter of my endeavors as a speaker, writer, and most importantly friend. Thanks to the highly skilled Brian Dawson for his awesome editing work. You can check out more of Brian's work on TheCASHFLOW.com (My entrepreneur family from which I belong to)

Thanks to my PR Team 5290 Media Group, under the guidance of Alean Elston.

Thanks to the designer and artist who helped to bring my vision to life! None other than Satyawan "Truth" Narinedhat. The countless revisions, and fluidity between us was amazing! Satyawan is a true professional and I am eager for our next project. Artistic is an understatement.

Thanks to Tiffany "The Budgetnista" Aliche for helping me to "Budget" my time by always being available to guide me during the process of troubleshooting when the book process was getting the best of me! With your deposits of advice and encouragement in my account... I didn't go bankrupt! Cha-Ching! (www.thebudgetnista.biz).

Thank you to Momma "Bren" You have opened your doors to me and treated me like the second son that you never had. I am forever grateful.

Thank you to Mr. Thorpe. If it were not for you believing in my vision to uplift and inspire I would NOT be where I am now. You shared advice and life lessons that have attached themselves to my soul and I am forever grateful. I will always remember to copyright my vision.

Mrs. Rocker-Brown for believing in me and pushing me to think bigger and to NEVER think of limits but rather adopt the mindset of NO CONFINES! There are lessons that you have unknowingly shared. You have shown me what it takes to renew your soul in the work of helping our youth and NEVER forgetting the reason you began…DAILY.

Mrs. Sesay, Thank you for listening to my rants and rambles about this creation to change the lives of our community and society. I thank you for sharing your wisdom and enthusiasm and NEVER looking at title but rather potential. I appreciate you.

Andre Stephens thanks for pushing me to write, write and continue to write. (DeepEndAquatics.com)

Much love to my Dream catcher family and extended family. I have received inspiration from you in many ways. Both known and unknown… Tiffany, Orane, Ediomi, Chike, Dreena, Dawn, Chaia, Uncle Wes, Lauren, Natay, Kareem, Deacon Dixon, Lindsey, Akintola, Diesa, Myradage, Valerie, Nina and our mentee Eshani Way and supportive family Dawn & Dean Way. My family of dreamcatchers embodies the essence of "it takes a village…" You all have touched my life in a substantial way and I am forever grateful.